Leadership skills
for success

Leadership skills for success

JEAN CIVIL

WARD LOCK

To Carl Brookes

A WARD LOCK BOOK

First published in the UK 1997
by Ward Lock
Wellington House
125 Strand
London
WC2 0BB

A Cassell Imprint

Distributed in the United States
by Sterling Publishing Co., Inc.
38 Park Avenue South, New York, NY 10016-8810

A British Library Cataloguing in Publication Data block for this book may be
obtained from the British Library

ISBN 0 7063 7703 6

Designed, edited and produced by Pardoe Blacker Publishing Ltd,
Lingfield, Surrey RH7 6BL

Printed in Hong Kong by Midas Printing Limited

CONTENTS

■ Chapter 3: Does my lifestyle preference affect my management style?

■ Chapter 4: How do I manage and lead my team?

Acknowledgements

I would like to thank all the hundreds of managers I have met over the years as a Management Trainer, for their quotes, insights and stories. Hearing your stories made it possible for me to know and write about managers.

A special thank you to Jeannie Turnock for her computer skills in typing this book, and particularly for her excited interest and constant encouragement while I was writing it.

I am indebted to Norman Dickie, my co-trainer, for the witty – even rude – comments he made when he read the first drafts. He really helped me to focus.

I would also like to thank some great trainers with whom I have worked, Derek Marsh, Brenda Mallon, Colin Turner, Pablo Foster, Diane Brace and the late Bill Pasquerella, for their expertise, insights and humour on our training ventures.

Thanks go particularly to Mike Bryan, Ray Masters and the staff at Network Training. Then there are all the managers who have managed ME! In particular two terrific ones: Alan Chitty and Liz Balinger.

I am so grateful to my agent Alan Gordon Walker, who gave me confidence and made it all happen, and the superb staff at Pardoe Blacker.

Finally, but really by no means least, to my son Carl who did some word processing and commented on the contents, and my husband Geoff, who supported me emotionally and physically throughout the months of continuous work involved.

INTRODUCTION

I remember many years ago being asked at my first interview for a management post, 'What would you say is your management style?' I didn't know. Oh, I knew that I related well to people and that I enjoyed my work and I was enthusiastic, keen and go-ahead. I was good at developing any ideas or projects assigned to me and made them happen. But I did not have any formal management qualification and I did not have any 'management speak'.

I did get the job, maybe because the same interviewer helped me out, as I froze, not knowing the answer, and added 'Would you say that you were ... or ...?'. Gratefully, I chose the option that seemed nearest to how I would like to be seen.

So if you are a manager and would like to know what your management style is, then this book is for you. I wish I had known about all the different management methods and many ways of gaining insight into my characteristics and management styles all those years ago. I would have been a better manager if I had. Trying to understand why staff behave in different ways from my style of management was difficult for me to comprehend. My intentions were to improve the quality of service to clients and the working practices of the staff, but although I gave the same instructions to individuals, they were perceived differently. Some staff would be with me, others against me, and the majority would be for or against me according to who they had just spoken to.

If you want to manage your staff positively, you will need to get to know their personal characteristics. You already know from experience what has motivated people in the past, what their idiosyncrasies are, their breaking points and in what they take delight. You will know what are their 'crumple buttons' (when they are hurt by criticism) and what are their 'chuff buttons' (when they are delighted at something you have said to them). The difficulty arises when staff behave in different ways from what you are expecting. Maybe you have a team meeting and someone becomes angry or upset about a certain issue, which seems out of character. So you have to explore the reasons for their reactions.

You may have to fill a new post and several members of your own staff apply, but there is only one position. So if five apply you motivate one and demotivate the other four. You will need lots of skills and knowledge to be able to remotivate them.

Or you may, as a leader, need to implement some changes but wonder how you can do this because most of the staff do not realize the pressures on you. You may have to produce a better service, improved product or become a more financially stable department or organization. How you bring about these changes will affect the organization, your staff, and your clients. Therefore it is necessary for you to know how to bring about positive change that is actively accepted by your staff.

Also, in the process of doing all these things, you will need to reduce the pressures on yourself in order to be an effective manager. All these aspects of leadership skills for success are explored and you are given opportunities to discover where your strengths and weaknesses lie.

Use this book as a step-by-step guide to recognizing your own management and leadership style and then see how you can best motivate and lead your staff in a personally fulfilling way. You may be surprised at what you will discover about yourself!

CHAPTER **1**

What are my personal characteristics?

You will probably find that you can manage some staff better than others and that you get on with, and relate more easily to, certain members of your team. There can be many reasons for this: one could be your own particular personality traits. Different personalities are a useful asset in your team: if you were all the same you would miss what other personalities can bring to it. You need to be able to identify the different characteristics that people exhibit. By recognizing individual styles of behaviour, you are more likely to understand how to lead people and motivate them to achieve a successful work force.

Begin by looking at *your* personal characteristics. By so doing you will also be able to identify some of the personal characteristics of your team and maybe your line manager.

This questionnaire is adapted from the work of David Keirsey and Marilyn Bates. I have called it 'The Civil cameo of characteristics', since it offers you a cameo, a small picture of yourself and others.

If you want to explore this area in greater depth, you could attend a workshop on Myers Briggs Types or see a counsellor or psychologist who is qualified to administer such psychometric tests. Contact BAC (British Association of Counsellors, Rugby) or BPS (British Psychological Society).

So begin discovering your own particular style of leadership and personal characteristics by completing Questionnaire 1.

The Civil cameo of characteristics

QUESTIONNAIRE 1

• •

Circle either the black star ★ or the white star ☆ in each of the 70 pairs of questions. Choose the option that is your most likely way of behaving, thinking or feeling. I realize that neither option may be exactly what you do, but choose the one *nearest* to what you would do. Please avoid thinking 'it depends'.

1   With other people, do you

    ★   like to keep ahead with what is happening

    ☆   tend to be the last to know what is happening

2   When asked to do something, that makes sense, do you

    ★   actually do it

    ☆   think of other ways it could be done

3   When working with instructions, do you

    ★   follow the instructions precisely

    ☆   do some guess work or take some short cuts

4   When reflecting on a new relationship, do you

    ★   consider what this may involve

    ☆   recall the warmth and touch

5 When meeting people, are you

★ thinking about what they do

☆ taking them at face value

6 When a final decision is reached, do you

★ accept it

☆ ask for it to be open for change

7 When dressing for some occasion, would you

★ organize what you will be wearing

☆ leave a few options open to decide at the time

8 Do you consider yourself

★ approachable

☆ reserved

9 Do you

★ live in the now

☆ look to the future

10 Children need

★ the practicalities of life

☆ opportunity to develop their imagination

11 Do you listen mostly to your

★ brain

☆ heart

12 When problem-solving, are you

★ reasoning what will be the cause and effect

☆ assessing the impact on the people involved

13 Of which do you most approve

★ a regulated and controlled life

☆ a flexible and spontaneous life

14 Do you prefer to be in a position of having

★ purchased

☆ your option still open to buy

15 With strangers, do you

★ make conversation easily

☆ find it difficult to know what to say

16 To which sort of person are you more readily attracted

★ practical

☆ imaginative

17 Is it more difficult for you to

★ identify with people

☆ use others

18 How would you prefer to be described

★ you are a rational person

☆ you are a sentimental person

19 Are you inclined to be

★ analytical

☆ sympathetic

20 When going to a meeting, are you
   ★ punctual
   ☆ leisurely

21 Do you feel more at ease
   ★ having made a decision
   ☆ still to come to a decision

22 Which do you consider is the nearest to your behaviour
   ★ liking to talk to people
   ☆ liking to write to people

23 When reading, do you prefer
   ★ factual prose
   ☆ abstract and figurative prose

24 Which do you prefer
   ★ focusing on what is actually possible
   ☆ focusing holistically on what might be possible

25 In which situation are you more at ease
   ★ discussing and debating an issue thoroughly
   ☆ coming to a consensus of agreement

26 Someone comes to you with a personal concern, do you
   ★ ask them what their options are
   ☆ empathize

27 Which statement is the nearest to describing you
   ★ avoid last-minute stresses
   ☆ feel energized by last-minute pressure

28 Do you
   ★ take your time to shop around for the best price
   ☆ buy things impulsively

29 When going into a new group, would you
   ★ talk freely to a lot of people
   ☆ keep yourself to yourself, only talking to one or two

30 Which would you rejoice most in having
   ★ experience
   ☆ inspiration

31 Do you tend to live
   ★ in the past
   ☆ in the future

32 Are you more comfortable when people talk about
   ★ their reasons for their relationship failing
   ☆ their feelings about the relationship failing

33 To reassure and make contact with someone would you
   ★ talk to them
   ☆ touch them

34 If money, status and qualification were the same, and you have to choose one of the two jobs, which would you most enjoy being

★ a lawyer

☆ a freelance writer

35 Would you feel more irritated if

★ a job was left unfinished

☆ a job was finished

36 Do you have

★ numerous friends and acquaintances

☆ a few close friends

37 When doing some tasks, do you

★ do it as it is usually done

☆ find a new way to please yourself

38 When reading books, do you prefer

★ straightforward language that gets to the point, and try to relate it to your experiences

☆ comparisons, analogies and symbolism, and try to forecast what might happen

39 When forming your opinions about people's misdemeanours, do you

★ set their behaviour against the law and rules

☆ wonder what were the circumstances that led to their behaviour

40 Which word do you use more often

★ logical

☆ value

41 Would you rather

★ have deadlines to meet

☆ be in a position to organize your own time

42 Would you say you

★ like to plan

☆ are adaptable

43 If the telephone rings, do you

★ rejoice that somebody wants to talk to you

☆ feel it is an intrusion on your time

44 Do you believe people need to

★ be observed, noticed and remembered

☆ interrelate and there is meaning in their relationships

45 Which is better

★ to know what you have to do practically

☆ to imagine what you could do given the chance

46 Which person would you commend

★ the rational thinking person

☆ the passionate, feeling person

47   Is it better to
   ★   be fair
   ☆   have mercy

48   How do you like events to happen
   ★   by making choices and selecting people
   ☆   by being spontaneous and involving anyone

49   Do you place importance on
   ★   defining arrangements
   ☆   leaving arrangements open

50   When telephoning, do you
   ★   dial the number and say what comes into your head
   ☆   plan what you have to say before dialling

51   Are you more influenced by
   ★   reality
   ☆   opinions

52   Are you interested more in
   ★   the simple meaning
   ☆   the hidden meaning

53   Which would you desire to be
   ★   a clear thinker
   ☆   a compassionate person

54   Which do you think you are
   ★   tough minded
   ☆   tender minded

55   Are you more relaxed if you
   ★   have signed a contract
   ☆   work on a casual basis when needed

56   Do you tend to
   ★   schedule your day
   ☆   be spontaneous to what may arise

57   At social gatherings do you tend to be the one that
   ★   enjoys the evening more as it goes on, reluctant to leave
   ☆   leaves earlier than others, feeling tired and thinking that you have had enough

58   Are you more
   ★   trusting of your experience than trusting of your inspiration
   ☆   trusting of your inspiration than trusting of your experience

59   Do you think that you can
   ★   actually and practically do things
   ☆   be trusted to do things in your own way

60   Would you like to be seen as
   ★   reasonable
   ☆   compassionate

61 Do you prize the quality in yourself that makes you

★ look for the truth

☆ able to create harmony

62 Would you think you have most in common with someone

★ who is organized and deals with precise details

☆ who just lets down their hair and reacts to circumstances

63 With which setting are you most at ease

★ something well structured and organized

☆ something unstructured and open-ended

64 Do you find being with new people in new situations

★ exciting and energizing

☆ nerve-wracking and tiring

65 Do you tend to

★ focus on what is practical

☆ play with the possibilities

66 Are you more inclined to

★ wonder what people could do for you

☆ wonder how people tick

67 When given information, do you

★ like to be given it step by step

☆ prefer to jump about the order and interrupt

68 If a partner were to let you down, would you prefer

★ to know the whole truth

☆ to try to harmonize the situation

69 Do you think a 'do gooder'

★ tends to break society's rules and make excuses for people

☆ helps people who are unable to help themselves

70 Do you believe rules are

★ to be obeyed

☆ to be used and adapted

How to score the Civil cameo of characteristics

The tables show you a list of question numbers with a black star ★ and a white star ☆ next to them. Go through your answers and *circle* the choice you made for each of the question numbers; (circle ★ or ☆). Then add up the number of *circles* for each column. To discover your E or I score you add up only one column, but to discover your S or N, T or F, J or P, score you add two columns together, as shown, to give you your grand total.

E or I score		
	E	**I**
1	★	☆
8	★	☆
15	★	☆
22	★	☆
29	★	☆
36	★	☆
43	★	☆
50	★	☆
57	★	☆
64	★	☆
total		

grand total   E   I

S or N score					
	S	**N**		**S**	**N**
2	★	☆	3	★	☆
9	★	☆	10	★	☆
16	★	☆	17	★	☆
23	★	☆	24	★	☆
30	★	☆	31	★	☆
37	★	☆	38	★	☆
44	★	☆	45	★	☆
51	★	☆	52	★	☆
58	★	☆	59	★	☆
65	★	☆	66	★	☆
sub total			**sub total**		

grand total   S   grand total   N

★   ☆

T or F score					
	T	**F**		**T**	**F**
4	★	☆	5	★	☆
11	★	☆	12	★	☆
18	★	☆	19	★	☆
25	★	☆	26	★	☆
32	★	☆	33	★	☆
39	★	☆	40	★	☆
46	★	☆	47	★	☆
53	★	☆	54	★	☆
60	★	☆	61	★	☆
67	★	☆	68	★	☆
sub total			sub total		

J or P score					
	J	**P**		**J**	**P**
6	★	☆	7	★	☆
13	★	☆	14	★	☆
20	★	☆	21	★	☆
27	★	☆	28	★	☆
34	★	☆	35	★	☆
41	★	☆	42	★	☆
48	★	☆	49	★	☆
55	★	☆	56	★	☆
62	★	☆	63	★	☆
69	★	☆	70	★	☆
sub total			sub total		

grand total [ ]   grand total [ ]   grand total [ ]   grand total [ ]

   T   F   J   P

   ★   ☆   ★   ☆

Now look at the four boxes where you scored highest to find your cameo of characteristics. For example, if you scored:

8	2	7	13	4	16	13	7
E	**I**	**S**	**N**	**T**	**F**	**J**	**P**

then you would have a cameo of **E N F J**.

What does my score mean?

Do managers have different characteristics?

There are sixteen possible permutations deriving from Questionaire 1 which are set out in the following table.

There are no absolute rights and wrongs, just differences. Each cameo has its own positive elements and also offers suggestions about how you could improve your leadership skills. First, I will give you a brief synopsis of what each letter means,

ENFP Imaginative and enthusiastic manager. Improvisor and quick to respond to requests. Good at new ideas and helping staff with their concerns.	**ENTP** Stimulating and outspoken manager. Good at solving challenging problems, seeing both sides of arguments and thinking through options.
ESTP Adaptive and tolerant manager. Likes excitement and quick explanations. Good at taking things apart and putting them back together.	**ESFP** Easy-going and friendly manager. Knows what is happening around you. Good at remembering facts and practical things.
INTJ Independent and determined manager. Great drive for your own ideas. Good at organizing a job and completing it without help.	**INFJ** Concerned and quietly forceful manager. Respected for your principles. Good at imagining new ideas and strategies to asssist staff.
ISTJ Practical and dependable manager. Make up your own mind as to what needs doing. Good at getting things done, being logical and organized.	**ISFJ** Responsible and stable manager. Quietly friendly and work devotedly to meet your obligations. Good at assessing how staff feel.

followed by a list of motivators for you at work. These will show how the characteristics may influence your leadership and management styles.

■ What do these letters stand for?

These cameos of characteristics are based on the idea that people have preferences that define the ways in which they feel most comfortable in their behaviour towards other people and situations.

ENFJ Sociable and responsive manager. Concerned about staff feelings. Good at leading group discussions and praising your staff.	ENTJ Knowledgeable and decisive manager. Like to organize and plan situations. Good at public speaking
ESTJ Realistic and practical manager. Solve problems and have a natural ability for business. Good at organizing and running activities.	ESFJ Conscientious and popular manager. When involved in meetings is likely to be good at doing practical things to help staff.
INTP Quiet, and an ideas manager. Reserved with theoretical interests. Good at solving problems and analyzing events in depth.	INFP Loyal and enthusiastic manager. Strive for harmony, work quietly on your own projects. Good at getting things done even when overworked.
ISTP Observant and analytical manager. Interested in how things work and cause and effect. Unexpected flashes of original humour.	ISFP Sensitive and modest manager. Kind, and you live in the 'now'. Like harmony. Good at being relaxed about getting things done.

The **E** stands for **E**xtroversion – the **I** for **I**ntroversion.
The **S** stands for **S**ensing – the **N** for I**N**tuition
The **T** stands for **T**hinking – the **F** for **F**eeling
The **J** stands for **J**udging – the **P** for **P**erceiving

Extrovert or introvert

Extroversion means directing your interest outward, towards the environment, its objects and people.

Introversion means directing your interest inwards to your own thoughts and feelings, valuing peace and solitude.

Examples of the differences are:

If you are extrovert you are likely to be	If you are introvert you are likely to be
Gregarious	Intimate
Enthusiastic	Quiet
Initiator	Receptor
Expressive	Contained
Auditory	Visual

So how does this relate to me at work?

If you are an extrovert you are likely to prefer	If you are an introvert you are likely to prefer
Working in groups	To talk on a one to one basis
Being in the spotlight	Working alone
Being sociable	Being reserved
Being open with people	Controlling what you say to people
Managing by talking to people	Managing by writing to people

The lists below give some of the behaviours and attitudes that I have adopted for this book to show how the research findings can be applied in practical management ways.

Extroversion	Introversion
You prefer the 'outer world' of people and things	You prefer to reflect on your 'inner world' rather than the outer world
You are active and involved with people	You prefer writing to talking
You gain energy from others	You may enjoy social contact but need to recover from it
You want to experience things in order to understand them	You want to understand something before trying it out
You work by trial and error	You tend to be persistent
You like a variety of work patterns	You like a quiet place in which to work

This does not mean that you only behave or think in one particular way, but that you are more likely to choose a particular way if given the choice.

There may be times as a manager, colleague or friend that you want to be involved with people, whereas at other times you may prefer solitude.

I gave this questionnaire to a management trainer with whom I have worked for many years and who I knew really well. As a bit of fun, I privately wrote down my perception of what his score would be. I was wrong and was surprised to find that his cameo came out as 'I' characteristic when I thought 'E'. But then as a management trainer, I only see his outgoing, people-orientated side, rather than his preference for introversion.

Sensing or intuition

What is meant by sensing and intuition?

Sensing   means gathering your information by way of your senses. Seeing, hearing, tasting, smelling, touching.

Intuition   means gathering your information by how you see the possibilities and meanings of relationships around you.

Sensing	Intuition
Like facts	See possibilities and patterns
Are realistic and practical	Are imaginative
Are observant about what is actually happening	Like to see the overall picture
Work steadily step by step	Work in bursts of energy with quiet periods in between and need inspiration
Enjoy owning things and making them work	Like a variety of things to do
Are patient and good with detail	Become impatient with routine jobs

Again if you have scored highly on one or other of these two dimensions then you may recognize some of your characteristics. By highly, I mean a difference in the score of more than six points. However, there may be times when you like facts and other times when you see possibilities and patterns. But it is what *you* think about your score that counts and what feedback you get from friends and colleagues.

Thinking or feeling

Now let us look at the differences between thinking and feeling styles.

Thinking   is how you prefer to arrive at your decisions. You will tend to be interested in cause and effect and to be objective.

Feeling   is when you prefer to make decisions through your value system, relationships with people, and is subjective. We have thousands of attitudes but only tens of values.

Thinking	Feeling
Are fair, firm and sceptical	Are warm, sympathetic, aware of your staff's feelings
Are analytical and logical	
Are brief and businesslike	Are trusting of colleagues
Are critical of mistakes and people	Enjoy pleasing others
	Need harmony in your working relationships
Have clear and consistent principles	Have clear and consistent values

Does it give you pleasure or concern to discover which of these two categories you fall into? If you came out wanting to 'please people', then you are more likely to have a greater F score than T score. But again, it is what you *think* or *feel* about the results that count and whether you can use this knowledge in your life at work or at home.

Judging or perceiving

Finally, the meaning of your judging and perceiving scores.

Judging   tends to indicate that you are concerned with making decisions, seeking completion, planning projects or organizing procedures.

Perceiving is associated with your being more receptive to the signals that you are picking up from people and situations.

Now see if you recognize some of your characteristics listed below.

Judging	Perceiving
Are decisive	Are curious
Are industrious and determined	Are flexible and tolerant
	Like to leave things open
Are organized and systematic	Pull things together at the last minute
Take deadlines seriously	
Like to have things decided and settled	Sample many more experiences than you could possibly use

Does your cameo of characteristics sit comfortably with you now that you know what the initials stand for? Or are there aspects with which you disagree?

Look at three of your letters and see which explanation fits you. You may recognize characteristics of some of your staff or your own line manager.

ISJ Introverted sensing You like to notice things and work on something useful to others, quietly, systematically, and in depth.

ESP Extroverted sensing You want to find excitement and fun in your working environment.

INJ Introverted intuition You imagine new ideas, systems and strategies and apply them.

ENP Extroverted intuition You find lots of new and stimulating possibilities and promote new ventures.

ITP Introverted thinking You need to analyze events or ideas in depth and create new designs, models and frameworks.

ETJ Extroverted thinking You tend to analyze, organize and control situations, solve problems by using established ideas and information and get results.

IFP Introverted feeling You strive to find harmony and a sense of order, through working quietly and individually on something that matters to you.

EFJ Extroverted feeling You feel it is important to help others to be happy.

Now complete the management questionnaire so that you can put the jigsaw of management styles together at the end of the book, in order to see the final picture of how you can be successful.

QUESTIONNAIRE 2
What is my management style?

Having read Chapter 1, complete the following statements:

My Civil cameo of characteristics is _____

_____

_____

This leads me to think that I

_____

_____

I was not surprised by

_____

_____

I was surprised by

_____

_____

Now read on to discover how your characteristics affect your leadership style and see if you agree or disagree with the result.

CHAPTER

2

What is my leadership style?

Which of the sixteen cameos makes the best kind of leader? None of them does because you are multi-faceted in your skills and this is just one small aspect of your ability. However, within these cameos there are indicators of how you might be relating to your staff and what particular skills you may be exhibiting. All of these cameos have positive attributes and can give you insight into how you may be more successful at work, strengths you should be aware of and aspects you need to improve and work on.

Leading people to be successful means getting people to do what you want them to, either in order to achieve tasks or to behave in a certain way. If that thought troubles you, you will need to work at recognizing how you can relate to staff in a more direct way.

Let us look at what you may tend to do, and what are your likely strengths and possible areas of difficulty.

Look at the following table to see what a combination of two of your letters tends to indicate about your leadership style.

Leadership style	
SP	Would indicate that you like excitement and adventure in your job. That you respond to crises and are flexible and enjoy freedom to decide for yourself.
SJ	You probably enjoy being responsible and useful in your organization. You like to pay attention to detail when you are planning projects. Also you offer, stability and security to your staff.
NT	Your score suggests that you are happy when developing new ideas and procedures. You have the ability to analyze, criticize and understand what is asked of you. You demonstrate competence.
NF	You work towards and appreciate harmony in your working day and in relationships. Self-development is important to you and you believe that it is essential to support other people.

What are your strengths and what areas do you need to work on?

Likely strengths	Areas on which to work
SP You are good at trouble-shooting, responding to crises, and you are flexible and able to negotiate.	You may not be paying enough attention to details, routine and long-term planning.
SJ You create stability, establish procedures and are responsible.	You could be reluctant to change, and feel a sense of uncertainty.
NT You are skilled at seeing and designing new systems and have high standards.	You could find it difficult to deal with staff's emotional problems and lots of crises. You probably do not praise your staff enough, if at all.
NF You are supportive and encouraging to your staff and recognize the importance of the way people work to different values and beliefs.	You are likely to avoid focusing on the task in hand or being purely objective in managing people. You may tend to avoid resolving conflict situations.

Having discussed your cameo, ask yourself if you recognize some of those traits in yourself. You will find positive aspects in all the types. If you are sceptical, ask your staff, colleagues, friends and partners if they find you behaving in such ways. This is another chance for you to develop from feedback.

Storytime

Before I proceed to give you any more information I would like you to suspend disbelief and complete the following exercise.

Exercise 1

● ●

Write a short story about your ideal organization.

Once upon a time _____

_____

_____

_____

_____

_____

_____

_____

_____

_____

_____

_____

_____

_____

Please complete your story before turning to the following pages.

What is your story about? See if you wrote about the things that I forecast under your grouping.

Your story is likely to contain some of the following attitudes:

STs	Your story will tend to emphasize control, bureaucracy and hierarchy.
SFs	Your story is likely to express the warm human aspects necessary within the organization.
NTs	Your story will probably address the broad issues and new ideas and new markets.
NFs	You may comment on the broad issues but you will also include human ideals; possibly you will dwell on the development of self and others rather than on your duty or your power.

What are you thinking or feeling about your experience of writing your story? Can you now read between the lines and identify your values? Maybe these are different from those of some of your staff.

Your leadership cameo

Now that you have recognized and understood the 'normal' personality differences, how do you see yourself as a manager?

What is your leadership style? Leadership usually means how do you manage. By example, by bullying, by encouraging, by fear, or by appreciating and motivating your staff.

All your staff need to be valued. Leadership means getting what you want from staff and achieving certain results, and to do this, you have to find a way to motivate your staff.

Most staff want to please their leader, for whatever motive. Hence you will have to demonstrate pleasure in their good work. For some of you that may be easy, but for others it will be more difficult. Are you a natural praiser of people's contributions and behaviour, or do you think they are just doing what they are paid to do? Has your cameo of characteristics given you an insight into your style?

Do my personal characteristics affect my leadership skills?

Look at your leadership style and consider how it can be affected by your characteristics. Which of the following do you think you are most likely to be?

Tick the relevant box that seems to fit your self image:

The visionary leader ☐

The traditional leader ☐

The negotiating leader ☐

The charismatic leader ☐

What do you think are the characteristics of a

Visionary leader _____

_____

Traditional leader _____

_____

Negotiating leader _____

_____

Charismatic leader _____

_____

Now look at the following explanations and see how close you are to knowing your own style of leadership.

The visionary leader

The NT manager/leader

■ The designer

Your strengths

You are the architect of change. Your sceptical approach means that you question everything. You have X-ray vision, so you can construct capably. You are happy designing new projects and you can see what needs to be done. When you go into an organization you can see power bases and power structures. Your managerial type is often intellectually ingenious and you can flourish in technical and administrative areas. You enjoy solving problems. You have 'self-power' awareness, so you don't need to be competitive.

With your staff

You are supportive. Staff follow you because your visionary ideas are contagious. Unfortunately, you are not a natural praiser of staff. You believe if someone does a good job, it is recognised, and that in itself should be taken as praise. You, yourself are likely to be embarrassed by praise. You are upset at errors, but you are very responsive to new ideas from colleagues. You are stimulated rather than weighed down by trying to solve staff problems. You will stand alone if you think you are right. You give your opinions if asked, but don't always convey what you are thinking. You get very annoyed when people speak on your behalf, but you don't always show it.

Your own need for support

You cannot bear someone making the same mistake twice. You are not interested in maintenance and dislike untangling foul-ups. You expect people to understand you the first time. You avoid saying the obvious in case you insult people's intelligence or you look naive. So you may have a communication problem and expect people to read your mind. Your audience may lose sight of the forest because they are trying to understand the trees.

Your team management

You would be an asset and essential on a senior management team. If a team does not have a visionary leader, then it will not flourish. You make theoretical contributions, have a belief and enthusiasm in the possibilities of people's ideas. This enthusiasm can be contagious. You can be as enthusiastic about other people's ideas as you are about your own. However, you may spend too much time planning and delay execution.

One thing you need to do to be a successful leader

Learn how to praise people. There is no substitute for the manager's praise. You know this, but you just don't do it enough.

The traditional leader

The SJ manager/leader

■ The stabilizer

Your strengths

You are decisive, follow through commitment, have common sense. You keep the traditions of the organization, maintaining a sense of belonging and permanence. You like the official office parties and rituals of present-giving for those who are leaving or retiring. You have a strong sense of responsibility.

Staff can count on you when you are in charge. They probably recognize your need to have things stabilized. You like people to get to the point quickly, so you may become irritated with 'wafflers'. You like steady, reliable people, so if staff deviate from procedures you would bring this to their attention. Make sure you do this in private not in public. You may find it difficult to praise staff. You probably prefer to give trophies or status titles as rewards.

Your own need for support

You are prone to Parkinson's Law – the law of domination of means over ends. You may become too hung-up on the law and rules and so create straightjackets. You may resist change. Maybe you feel indebted to society and want to put something back into it. You need hard workers around you whom you can admire.

Your team management

You run efficient team meetings. They have well-ordered agendas and you pay attention to detail. You supply an effective smooth-running system. You would be necessary in a senior management team to ensure that details are not overlooked.

One thing you need to do to be a successful leader

You probably need to work on your people skills, especially those of helping or counselling.

The negotiating leader

The SP manager/leader

■ The practical diplomat

Your strengths

You will get jobs done, unafraid to challenge but also able to be adaptable. You will deal with the issue in hand but can also be spontaneous. A superb negotiator, you welcome and seek change in areas that can be changed and are negotiable such as policies, procedures and personnel.

With your staff

You are flexible and open-minded and able to take instructions from your line manager. You easily give appreciation and warm support to your staff. You do not judge your staff but accept their differences.

Your own need for support

As you live in the now you may forget commitments made in the past or for the future. You could become rigid if you are not involved in bringing about change in which you can negotiate. You could be unpredictable to your staff.

Your team management

You are an excellent team leader for initiating action and change. You work at, and believe in, giving staff pleasant working conditions.

One thing you need to do to be a successful leader

Organize staff around you to remind you of the other aspects of your work, like the unpleasant jobs.

The charismatic leader

The NF manager/leader

The participative democrat

Your strengths

Your skills are in relating to people. You have personal charisma and commitment to your staff. You have good interpersonal skills and often become deeply involved with the people with whom you work. You have a concern for both their careers and their personal development. You draw out and activate individuals. You have very good verbal skills. You are an excellent active listener and natural empathizer. Possibly you can make everyday dull events into something interesting and special. You are an optimist.

With your staff
You try to develop their potential. If your staff have personal concerns or issues, you will help them to handle them. You are an outstanding praiser of your staff when you believe they have worked well. You empower your staff, you enjoy being with them and you make business your pleasure.

Your own need for support
People's concerns and issues may sap your energy levels because you put so much of yourself into supporting and helping them. You need praise for your work. You are likely to put other people's needs before your own. You may become tired of the amount of people-involvement and you dislike formal, authoritative people.

Your team management
You are a natural democratic leader. You look for the best in each member of your team. You are likely to prefer unstructured meetings. You would be necessary in a senior management team to ensure that it is people-centred. Without you, the organization could be dull and joyless.

One thing you need to do to be a successful leader
You need to review your priorities. Try to avoid creating dependency relationships. Look after yourself in terms of health and give yourself some selfish time.

QUESTIONNAIRE 3

• •

What is my management style?

What do you now consider is part of your management style?

My leadership style is _____

This means that my strengths are

_____

_____

To be successful I need to consider working on

_____

_____

I connect with certain aspects of the explanations, which are

_____

_____

I do not see myself as described in the following ways

_____

_____

Now continue reading through the following chapters to discover other ways of looking at your management style and
working towards being a successful leader.

CHAPTER 3

Does my lifestyle preference affect my management style?

I believe that your attitude to life, your values, the way you think and feel, and how you are motivated will certainly affect the way in which you manage other people. More importantly, do *you* think that they do?

In order to find out if you are affected by your life preferences, first complete Questionnaire 4. When you have discovered your score and read the analysis, you can then assess whether your performance really does show these managerial strands.

Please do not read the analysis first, as this will certainly affect how you respond to the statements.

It is important to remember there are hundreds of different management questionnaires in circulation, and this one will highlight just one particular facet of your management style.

As before, there are no right or wrong answers. All the styles that emerge have positive attributes. You are not out to impress anyone, so be honest with yourself. That is the only way to get the most out of this experience. You may become delighted, thoughtful, surprised or aware. Maybe you will even change your management style. Thousands of managers have used this questionnaire with me and the results have been most revealing, so go ahead and see what happens...

QUESTIONNAIRE 4
Lifestyles

● ●

How to complete the questionnaire
Work through the following twenty-four statements. Work fairly quickly. Do not go back and look or check what you have written for previous statements. Try to use the range of scores appropriately as to their relevance. Allocate a score for *every* statement in the following way:

If you agree with the statement

completely	then allocate	5
to a large extent	allocate	4
moderately	allocate	3
to a small extent	allocate	2
not at all	allocate	1

▇ Statement

1   I prefer to be completely free to decide for myself how I want to live and be. ☐

2 In deciding how I want to live and be I prefer it if I have some family members, close friends or colleagues to help me reach this decision. □

3 I believe my life will be most satisfying if I have some clear pathways for advancing and being rewarded. □

4 I believe my life will be most satisfying if I have complete choice in how I want to live. □

5 I place a lot of faith in what my close friends say to me. □

6 I place a lot of faith in the law and order. □

7 I can only have the really important things in my life by doing what I want to do. □

8 I can only have the really important things in life by working closely with my friends and colleagues. □

9 What is important to me is that I have a secure job and a good home. □

10 What is important to me is that I gain personal growth through discovering who and what I am. □

11 What I do seems right when I am guided by the close relationships I have with other people. □

12 What I do seems right when I am guided by established norms and policies of the society in which I live. □

13 I am satisfied when my actions are guided by my own knowledge of what I want to do. □

14 I am satisfied when actions are guided by consultation with others who are close to me. □

15 I find myself wanting greater advancement and prestige. ☐

16 I find myself wanting greater freedom and independence to express myself. ☐

17 I believe life would be better for me if my colleagues and I were friendly and got on together. ☐

18 I believe the world would be a better place for me if people respected and abided by our established laws. ☐

19 I believe I should experience all of my feelings and emotions to the fullest extent. ☐

20 I believe my feelings and emotions should be shared with others who are close to me ☐

21 I am responsible for my actions to those in a position of higher authority to me. ☐

22 I am responsible to myself for my actions. ☐

23 I can grow and progress best in this world by learning and sharing with other people. ☐

24 I can grow and progress best in this world by finding out and knowing the way in which things ought to be done. ☐

■ How to score

Put your scores against the following statement numbers 1–24. For example, if you scored 4 for statement 1, then put a 4 in the scoring column next to Qu1:

Now total your scores in the three separate columns:

QU	SCORE	QU	SCORE	QU	SCORE
1		2		3	
4		5		6	
7		8		9	
10		11		12	
13		14		15	
16		17		18	
19		20		21	
22		23		24	
Total		**Total**		**Total**	

This is your personalistic score (**P**)

This is your sociocentric score (**S**)

This is your formalistic score (**F**)

Lifestyle preferences – analysis

Remember, this is not a personality test, it is all about life preferences, so you would have different personalities within these three lifestyles. How did you score? You may have found that you had a higher score in one of the three areas: personalistic, sociocentric or formalistic. These terms are described more fully later in this chapter. What you need to look at is the difference between the three scores.

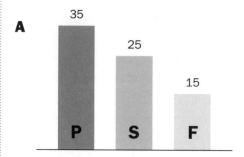

For example, if you had 35 in 'P', 25 in 'S' and 15 in 'F', you would need to concern yourself about the formalistic rules and organizational issues that are part of your job.

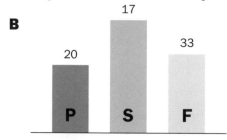

If you had 18 in 'P', 30 in 'S' and 21 in 'F' then you are likely to prefer working in groups and teams, but you may have to work on self-empowerment and occasionally being more assertive.

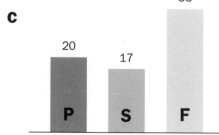

Whereas if you had 20 in 'P', 17 in 'S' and 33 in 'F', the differences would indicate that you are likely to be formalistic and probably need to pay more attention to your 'people' skills. It is likely that you would be more comfortable with the paper aspect of your job than the staff interaction your job requires.

The differences between scores would also indicate that you may be relying too much on the organization's rules, and waiting until you are told to do things before you initiate them.

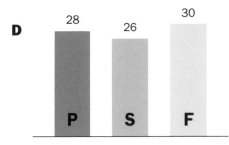

If, however, you had 28 in 'P', 26 in 'S' and 30 in 'F', then although 'F' is your highest score, the overall similarity in the scores would indicate that you are skilled in all three areas. You are capable of dealing with people in an empowering way, of working effectively in a team, and are quite comfortable handling almost all aspects of paperwork relating to the organizational structure in which you operate.

This is not to say that the latter score is the best (let us call this score 'M' for MIXED). It simply means that you are able to move from group to group and do not have any one strong preference. If, for example, you were working with a group of personalistic staff, you could become quite formal in your managerial style. If, on the other hand, you were working with a number of sociocentric people who were happier working within a group, you might want either to withdraw, or become very determined and outspoken if their views did not coincide with yours. If you were with a group of formalistic people, you might become really irritated by their emphasis on the rules and the organization's needs, and you would lean towards talking in terms of people's needs rather than structured procedures. So you are very adaptable.

It is important to recognize that you could have a high

personalistic score but not necessarily be an extrovert, while many personalistic people may be outgoing and speak their minds. Equally you could have a very quiet, introverted person who is equally personalistic and empowers themselves, thinking that they won't bother to say anything because they know what to do anyway and it is really a waste of their time because they know what is right.

If you have a difference of more than 7 points between your scores, you will need to look at your low-scoring areas and try to develop those particular aspects of your managerial style. If you have a low 'P' score, you will need to work at being more assertive and empowering yourself; if a low 'S' score you will need to work at being concerned about the maintenance of people's needs and becoming more warm and supportive; or if a low 'F' score you should recognize that your paper skills probably need some attention, perhaps you need to work at time management or personal organization or creating a balance between people and paper.

Now most people have the capacity to operate in all three styles, and you may be able to switch from one to the other depending on the sort of people with whom you are working. However, this exercise may suggest that you have one, or maybe two, preferred styles which you tend to use. Be aware of this and recognize that it may be to your advantage as a manager to develop the ability to work comfortably within the third style. It would be silly to deny your aptitudes, but if you are hoping to manage people as well as you possibly can, you need to find a job that allows you to operate in your preferred style otherwise you may become very superficial or frustrated.

Questionnaires such as this can work for most people, but there is a small number for whom this particular technique just does not work. If this seems true for you, check with your staff which style they think you adopt.

The personalistic style

If your management style is personalistic, your strength lies in the way in which you make known your beliefs and what you want from your staff. You have some very good points because you believe in empowering yourself, and you are likely to manage your staff in such a way that they feel a similar sense of personal worth and empowerment, which enables them to work on their own initiative without constantly seeking the authority to do so, and without fear of reprisal.

However, if some of your staff have a formalistic life preference, they will want you to tell them exactly what the rules are, how to do things, and by when.

Your reference point is yourself and how you feel, what your ideals are and your beliefs. Your main concern is to develop yourself as an individual and find your full potential. You are bored by rules, regulations and systems of procedure. Also, you find people in groups are comparatively unimportant compared with how you feel about yourself and your job.

You will probably fight for the strong views which you hold, and rather than reach some sort of compromise you would prefer to stay in the minority position. If you do not believe in something, then you cannot really be bothered supporting it. Because you don't bother about rules you are probably a terrific innovator and creative thinker.

So your strengths are that you will stand up for what you believe in, you have lots of new ideas, you do not mind taking risks, and you are unlikely to be very career-minded. If you do not believe in a particular code, you are unlikely to be interested in it, and if targets are set you need to have them made very clear to you, otherwise you will be uninterested in getting the work done.

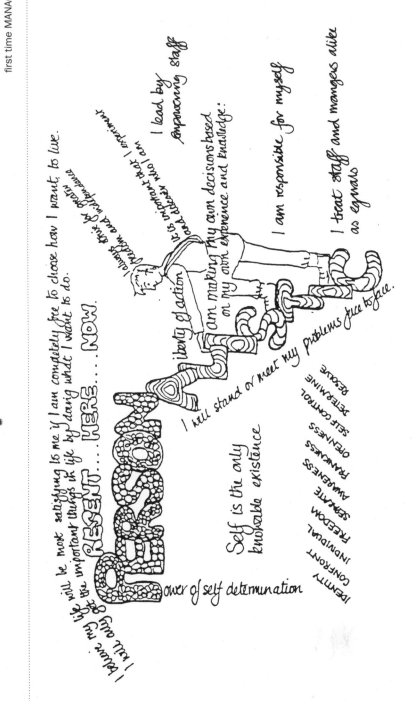

I lead by empowering staff

I am responsible for myself

I treat staff and manages alike as equals

it is important that I experience
it is important that who I am

liberty of action

I am making my own decisions based
on my own experience and knowledge.

I will stand or meet my problems face to face.

Self is the only
knowable existence

IDENTITY
CONFRONT
INDIVIDUAL
FREEDOM
SEPARATE
AWARENESS
FRANKNESS
OPENNESS
SELF CONTROL
DETERMINE
RESOLVE

PRESENT . . . . HERE . . . . NOW.

I will be most satisfying to me if I am completely free to choose how I want to live.
by doing what I want to do.

I believe my life will be the important things in life only
I will only

power of self determination

However, your weakness could be that you are so inner-concerned that you could become self-centred. You may find it difficult to listen to what other people have to say, and maybe you do not appear to value their contributions at meetings or in staff rooms. If you are not interested in what is being discussed, you will refuse to take part, withdraw, or you may even leave the room.

You like direction from within and believe in what you think is right, or needed. You like the freedom of self-control, to decide for yourself what you are going to do, and you feel responsible to yourself. You like to empower other people, you hate not being yourself and you take material goods very much for granted.

You are an idependent individual who identifies with other individuals rather than an organization and your feelings and emotions must be experienced to the full. Change occurs for you by addressing issues and people and you live in the 'now'. You are usually a fun person to have around, provided you are interested in what is going on.

Personalistic people, with their innovative ways and their ability to challenge systems and procedures are needed within an organization.

The sociocentric style

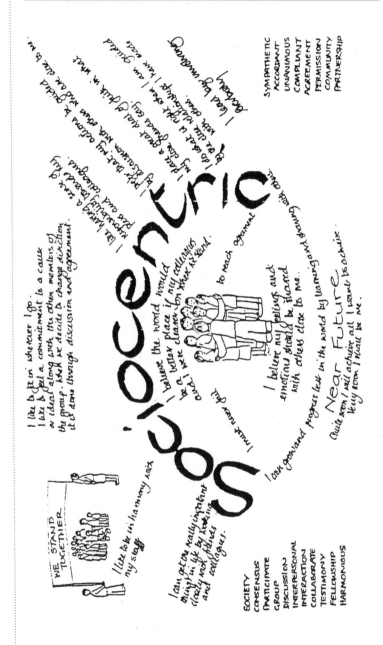

If your scoring has shown that you have a strong tendency towards being sociocentric, you will tend to look towards other people and groups as a reference point for yourself. You will probably be concerned to make groups work, both within and outside of the workplace. You are supportive, you like people, you probably smile a lot and you would want to have people's permission and support before you went out on a limb with a new idea.

Group relations are more important to you than the task, and if you are strongly sociocentric you will probably be skilled and sensitive at handling group behaviour and understanding about group dynamics, probably operating in informal rather than formal settings. Your particular strength is holding a group together and acting as an excellent facilitator.

You are also probably good at checking whether everyone has agreed with a decision, and you make sure that people in your team, or your colleagues who may be quiet, are coaxed into any discussions.

Your possible weakness is that you give too much credence to other people's ideas and don't spend enough time on your own sources of ideas and feelings. You are likely not to be very goal directed. Although the well-being of the group is extremely important to you, you may be comparatively unin-terested in actually getting the task done.

Organizations need the SOCIOCENTRIC member of staff, or manager, since you will be concerned about the welfare, the feelings and the relationships of staff and will want to consult them in order to ensure that everyone feels they have some kind of say in decision-making. If this is your preferred style, you are likely to be the one who arranges the Christmas out-ing, suggests collections for flowers, collects the coffee money, joins the staff for lunch breaks, and probably also socializes with colleagues outside work.

The formalistic style

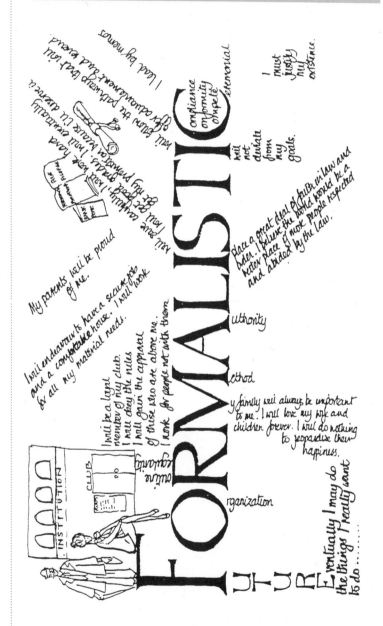

If you identify with this particular type, then you will tend to look for outside structures and outside rules by which to live, both at work and in your life in general. You want to know where you are going and have clear objectives, knowing the rules and looking for agreed ways of handling things and people.

You probably like working through tasks systematically and formally, and you may get impatient with irrelevances or people's interruptions. You are generally good working within an organization, being supportive and often creating good operating systems. Your strengths lie in your power to have clear goals, with direct thinking and working. You are likely to be particularly good at dealing with large quantities of paperwork and information, and co-ordinating things systematically so that all the rules are met.

You probably have a tidy desk. Your staff know what is expected of them in terms of procedures. You are good at taking and producing minutes. You are likely to be concerned about status and titles. You probably work 'for' people rather than 'with' people.

However, your weaknesses may be your over-attachment to formal procedures, combined with an unwillingness to take risks and try new approaches, or to talk with groups in order to bring forward new ideas. You may also be suspicious of people who do not always work within the organization's rules and it is highly likely that your views will be conservative and traditional.

Notices put up on the notice board by the formalistic person would probably have four drawing pins, one in each corner, while the personalistic manager would probably put a notice over somebody else's with just one drawing pin in the middle! Sociocentrics, of course, wouldn't bother with a notice at all – they would just go around telling everybody.

Your major values and how you manage

Your values	Personalistic
Your are stimulated by	Direction from within
Your form of control	Is based on what you think is right or needed
You are motivated and are given the incentive to work	By having freedom, self-control, order to decide things by yours•
You feel responsibility towards	To yourself
Your desired end is	To empower staff
You try to avoid	Not being yourself
In order to gain material goods you	Take them for granted
Your basis for growth is to	Raise your self-awareness
You see yourself as	A separate individual
You identify with and are loyal to	An individual
Your feelings and emotions are likely	To be totally experienced
Change occurs for you by	Addressing issues and people
You live in	The now

:iocentric	Formalistic
scussion and agreement with ners	Direction from authoritive figures
by interpersonal mmitments	Is by rules, laws and policies
approval and group or team hesion	By money, status, grades, prestige, advancement
your peers, colleagues	Your line manager and the organization
reach agreement	To comply
ilure to reach agreement with ur colleagues	Deviating from the rules of authoritative figures
llaborate	Compete
eract with others	Follow the rules of the organization
peer group member	A member of the hierarchy
group	The organization
be shared with a few close lleagues	To be analyzed and channelled
ving group discussions volving your staff	Being given direction, influence and manoeuvre
e near future	The future

How did you score?

Now draw in your bar chart – put a line for your score in the relevant box.

Finally, if you have a predominant score in one particular area, you will probably need to consider developing your skills in the other two areas. For instance, if your 'P' score is high, try to involve your staff more in decisions and pay attention to your administration. If your 'S' score is high, aim to be more individual and keep up to date with your paperwork. If your 'F' score is high, then remember that talking to people is more rewarding than communicating through memos. While you can recognize your preferred style and realize that it is in your best interests to develop your skills in other areas, it would be totally unwise to deny your naturalness

Now link your cameo of characteristics with your lifestyle scores.

	Personalistic P	Sociocentric S	Formalistic F
Extrovert E	**PE** Say what you think	**SE** Organizes parties	**FE** Outgoing, talker of rules
Introvert I	**PI** Don't bother to voice an opinion, know you are right	**SI** Make a few close friends, lots of acquaintances	**FI** Writes direct memos
Sensing S	**PS** Organize individual work areas	**SS** Ask people what equipment they need to do their job	**FS** Enjoy taking the minutes at a meeting
Intuitive N	**PN** Empower staff and believe in their individual worth	**SN** Know when someone in your team is hurt or angry	**FN** Forecast people's responses to your directives
Feeling F	**PF** There to help if someone needs support	**SF** Ask your team how they feel about situations	**FF** Empathize with how instructions affect staff
Thinking T	**PT** Focused, bright, challenges ideas	**ST** Think about the importance of staff involvement	**FT** Know the formal procedures of committee meetings and policies
Perceptive P	**PP** Can visualize holistically the potential of staff and the organization	**SP** Perceive the staff as needing to be valued	**FP** Perceive how staff are likely to respond to change
Judgemental J	**PJ** Judge people openly on the misuse of power, either by speaking or writing to them	**SJ** Judge the behaviour of people who ignore the feelings of others	**FJ** Decide on and enforce laws, rules and policies

WHAT IS MY MANAGEMENT STYLE?
Personal awareness exercise
● ●

My personalistic score is _____

My sociocentric score is _____

My formalistic score is _____

Having read the explanations I think that my management style is

_____

_____

My strengths are

_____

_____

_____

I need to work on

_____

_____

_____

_____

When you have read the whole book, you will be able to recognize your various managerial styles. These are likely to emerge even though I have used very different kinds of managerial views and management models.

CHAPTER **4**

How do I manage and lead my team?

The best and simplest way to find out how you manage your team, is to ask them: this in itself would indicate that you are managing them positively. If you do ask them, realize that the responses will contain as many different perceptions as you have team members, for each one is likely to have differing needs and expectations, both of you as their manager and also of their team.

I expect within your team you have favourites. They may be those you can depend on, or those you can have a laugh with, but it is most likely to be those whom you can trust. Many years ago an international management consortium paid consultants to do research into what made a 'great team'. After a lot of time and money was spent on the project they came up with the vital ingredient – TRUST.

As a leader do I need to develop trust in my team?

Yes. Whatever your present leadership style, you will also need to trust in, and to be trusted by, your team.

One of the most important features of a good team is the level of trust between its members. That means that they rely on each other and are willing to share information and feelings in the belief that they will be used for the good of the team as a whole and for the individual members. One of the functions of a team leader is to foster such trust. To do that you will need:

Confidence

Staff must know that risk-taking and normal human weakness will not be punished. Some of your staff may be afraid to disclose their own fears and inadequacies to you or others, in case they are ridiculed.

Self-disclosure

Your staff are more likely to trust other colleagues who are open about themselves, admitting weakness and fears, celebrating strengths and aspirations. In a good team, members are willing to express such feelings. Many staff may withhold personal information about themselves.

Time

Most staff have fears about their own vulnerability and require time to establish how far they can trust others not to hurt them. You may need to be patient.

To demonstrate   Most staff respond to a demonstration of trust by others and will reciprocate by being more open and trusting. As a good leader, you will need to demonstrate trust.

Feedback skills   Staff can only develop if they receive information about how you and their colleagues perceive their actions. Giving open, honest and constructive feedback is a means of generating trust between you and your staff.

■ In what ways can I create trust in my team?

Trust is essential – but be warned, once it is broken, it can never return to the same level as before, even though both people try hard to regain it. You can best create trust if you follow these rules:

1   Openly express your feelings and thoughts, especially when asked. Present them as statements about yourself, not criticism of others; for example, 'I don't agree with that suggestion', *not* 'That sounds a stupid idea'.

2   Listen to others' self-disclosure caringly: give them your full attention and *avoid* being judgmental or *identifying* with them; for example, 'I know how you feel, that happened to me' (only it was worse for me).

3   Let others know when you are uncertain or fearful. Ask for help when you need it; for instance, 'I am really anxious about addressing so many people at the public meeting'.

4   Give praise freely when it is earned; for example, 'I think you did a wonderful job on that project'. Feedback is not just for giving constructive criticism.

5   If you want to offer feedback, check that it is wanted, so preface it with, 'Would you like some feedback?'

6   Give feedback when asked. Present it as a gift for growth; offer only feedback that can be used to improve performance, for example, 'I think you presented your views with great conviction. However, I believe it would have been even more effective if you had ...'

7   Invite feedback from others, ask 'How am I doing?' Thank others when they give you feedback, even if you don't agree with it or like it. Try not to justify your behaviour. Just listen to what they are saying. It is their true perception of you.

8   Treat everything said to you as confidential unless it is clearly public knowledge; say 'I will treat what you have told me about your situation as confidential. If asked, I shall tell people to ask you'.

9   Check for hidden agendas. Do so openly; for instance, 'During the meeting I sensed that you were angry with me. It might be my imagination, but I'd like to check it out with you'.

10 Remember that most people do what they do for positive reasons. Look for positive intent and acknowledge it, even if you disagree with it; say 'I am sure that your intentions were good, thank you for trying to solve the problem'.

How can I identify positive and negative behaviour?

You can achieve this by being aware of what is positive behaviour in teams and bringing your staff around to recognizing that there are certain ways in which the team must behave.

Are you an optimist or a pessimist? As a pessimist you will find the negative aspects of people and situations, while as an optimist you are more likely to see the good points in your staff.

Behaviour that is regarded as negative usually includes bullying, calculating, dictating, protecting, censoring, clinging, avoiding involvement, judging and moaning.

Behaviour that is seen as positive within a team or relationship is initiating, integrating, goal-setting, clarifying, addressing, gaining agreement, evaluating and involving others.

You need to work at re-enforcing positive behaviour with your team. Also, as a manager, you need to recognize people's negative behaviour and move them to more positive interactions.

Nobody's perfect, but a team can be

Meredith Belbin, a well-known expert in team roles, said at a recent conference, 'Nobody's perfect, but a team can be…'. He identifies the following different team roles.

These are his most recent categories:

Plants	(Creative)
Resource investigators	(Develop contacts)
Monitor/evaluators	(Judge accurately)
Co-ordinators	(Promote decision making)
Shapers	(Challenging and dynamic)
Team workers	(Co-operative)
Implementors	(Put ideas into practice)
Completer/finishers	(Deliver on time)
Specialists	(Single-minded)

Ideally, teams need to contain a mixture of people in these roles in order to function at maximum efficiency. Some team members are able to change their major role if the team is lacking a certain category. For example, if there were no 'Completer/finisher' someone else might take this on. If they didn't, then as a team you would never get anything finished, and would just go around in circles.

Think subjectively about *your* team. Have you got people in these roles? Or are you missing some important element for success? You may like to consider who in your team best fits these roles.

Of course, you may use other names for your team members, as I have, and see their roles in a different way.

It doesn't matter what you call them, but it does matter that you have a mixture of recognizable skills on which you can concentrate. Try to give the right jobs to the right people.

The innovator
Comes up with ideas

The relator
Involves people

The judge
Passes a verdict

The equaliser
Believes all have rights

The challenger
Addresses comments

The ruler
Wants it on paper

The nit picker
Finds fault

The smarty pants
Shows off

The individualist
Does their own thing

The carer
Looks after everybody

Is my team effective?

Now look at your team, or one of your teams, and see how it compares with an effective team.

To know if your team is as effective as it could be you will need to consider the next ten key points.

1 Select appropriate jobs to get the best out of your team.

2 Select a mixture of people in terms of skills, specialities, interests, styles of working and thinking.

3 Provide time, space and money to set up your team.

4 Develop a team by looking for a good team-builder trainer.

5 Assist and work at moving your team from being ineffective to effective.

6 Change the staff in the team when necessary.

7 Change the jobs when necessary.

8 Support the team by valuing its work and empowering it to make suggestions and decisions.

9 Handle any team conflict.

10 Co-ordinate the work of all your teams if you have more than one.

Now try to assess how your team is doing. When you have completed the chart, offer it to a colleague for their perception of how they see the team. In fact all the members of your team could complete the chart and compare notes.

Instructions: Provide a rating from 1 (low) to 10 (high) by circling the number you think is most descriptive of your team.

1	**Trusting**
	Team members trust each other
	1　2　3　4　5　6　7　8　9　10

2	**Accepting**
	Team members are friendly, concerned and interested in each other
	1　2　3　4　5　6　7　8　9　10

3	**Addressing conflict**
	Team members acknowledge and address conflict openly
	1　2　3　4　5　6　7　8　9　10

4	**Listening**
	Team members listen with understanding to each other
	1　2　3　4　5　6　7　8　9　10

5	**Including everyone**
	Team members include others in the decision-making process
	1　2　3　4　5　6　7　8　9　10

6	**Supporting**
	Team members support and help each other
	1　2　3　4　5　6　7　8　9　10

7	**Achieving**
	Team members contribute ideas and solutions to issues and concerns
	1　2　3　4　5　6　7　8　9　10

8	**Appreciating**
	Team members value the contributions and ideas of others
	1　2　3　4　5　6　7　8　9　10

9	**Congratulating**
	Team members recognize and say well done to other team colleagues
	1　2　3　4　5　6　7　8　9　10

10	**Happy**
	Team members feel happy in the team
	1　2　3　4　5　6　7　8　9　10

How do I see my team and how can I support them?

Now rate your team in terms of their present performance (**P**), and your desired performance (**D**). On the scales below place **P** (your 'a' score) representing **present**, and a **D** (your 'b' score), representing **desired**, over the number which best represents how you:

(a)   see the team (put a P) and,

(b)   wish to see the team (put a D)

First work through all ten sections using P before assessing the D ratings.

1 is low and 10 is high

1 Objectivity Are we objective in the way we tackle things? We are never objective	1 2 3 4 5 6 7 8 9 10	We are always objective
2 Information We never obtain and use the necessary information	1 2 3 4 5 6 7 8 9 10	We always obtain and use all necessary information
3 Organization Our organization is never suitable for the tasks we have to perform	1 2 3 4 5 6 7 8 9 10	Our organization is always fully suitable for the tasks we are performing
4 Decision-making Our decision-making methods are always inappropriate	1 2 3 4 5 6 7 8 9 10	We always make decisions in the most appropriate way
5 Participation Participation is always at its lowest	1 2 3 4 5 6 7 8 9 10	Everyone participates fully

6 Leadership We are never led (managed) in an appropriate way	1 2 3 4 5 6 7 8 9 10	Our leadership (management) is highly appropriate
7 Bondability We have people who are disliked	1 2 3 4 5 6 7 8 9 10	We all like each other
8 Openness Opinions are never expressed openly	1 2 3 4 5 6 7 8 9 10	Opinions are always expressed openly
9 Use of time We always use time badly	1 2 3 4 5 6 7 8 9 10	We always use time well
10 Enjoyment We never enjoy our work	1 2 3 4 5 6 7 8 9 10	We always enjoy our work

Is there much difference between your P and D scores? If so, what can you do to bring your P scores nearer to your D scores? Discuss your perceptions with your team.

List one idea for each of the ten aspects:

1 **Objectivity** _____

2 **Information** _____

3 **Organization** _____

4 **Decision-making** _____

5 **Participation** _____

6 **Leadership** _____

7 **Bondability** _____

8	Openness	_____
9	Use of time	_____
10	Enjoyment	_____

How can I get my team to make decisions?

Here are six steps you can follow.

Step 1 Ask 'What do we need from this team?' List the needs, share comments and reflect upon them.

_____

_____

_____

Step 2 What is the real issue? Concentrate on one or two issues or concerns that your team needs to address. Now write them down.

_____

_____

_____

Step 3 What are the options open to us to achieve our needs and resolve the real issue? List these by brainstorming and when completed get the team to agree on which two will work.

_____

_____

_____

_____

Step 4   Which options do we choose? Everyone must agree on this.

_____

_____

_____

Step 5   What do we now have to do to meet our needs?

_____

_____

_____

Step 6   DO IT! Who does what, and by when?

_____

_____

_____

Team phases

Teams go through phases.

Think:

Forming	or	Ritual sniffing
Norming	or	Polite processing
Storming	or	In-fighting
Re-forming	or	Addressing attitudes
Performing	or	Maturing
Mourning	or	Disbanding

About three-fifths of the way through any team meeting you will have some storming. Accept this as inevitable, recognizing that if people get things off their chests they will perform better. Give them permission to air their views. Do not avoid feelings or they will fester.

Remember it is OK for staff to make mistakes. Give them permission to say what they think without fear of retribution. If a team has been together for a long time, keep your eye on the possibility of their becoming complacent. Check that they all know what is expected of them.

How can I establish and lead a superteam?

The ten behaviours of a superteam
It is difficult to state clearly what distinguishes an ordinary team from a superteam, but the following behaviours and feelings are only found in superteams, or high-performance teams.

1 People smile, genuinely and naturally.

2 There is plenty of laughter – genuine belly-laughs as opposed to nervous, embarrassed laughter.

3 People are confident – a 'can do' rather than 'can't do' group.

4 They are loyal to their team and to each other, addressing and resolving any conflict between them; they do not denigrate colleagues or the organization.

5 They are relaxed and friendly, not tense and hostile.

6 They are open to outsiders and interested in the world about them.

7 They are energetic, lively and active.

8 They are enterprising, taking the initiative rather than reacting to events.

9 They listen to, and do not interrupt, each other.

10 They check out what they have to do as individuals before the next team meeting.

Criteria for effective and superteams

1   Trust and support.

2   Clear objectives and agreed goals and procedures.

3   Open lines of communication.

4   The knowledge that conflict is inevitable but that it needs to be addressed.

5   The skills to deal with emotions and feelings openly: remember 'feelings are facts'.

6   Flexible leadership which is appropriate to its membership.

7   Progress meetings to celebrate successes and to ask for others' support in the areas of difficulty.

8   Concern with the personal and career development of its members.

9   A positive attitude when relating to the teams.

10 Recognition of the value of the individual strengths that each member brings to the team.

An effective team achieves its objectives and stays together, but a superteam has excellent people skills, success without stress and creatively achieves desired goals through members' trust and confidence in each other.

How can I maintain a superteam?

The ten characteristics of a superteam
The key properties and performance characteristics of the super-team suggest an ideal towards which teams should work and also provide a set of criteria against which to measure the effectiveness of existing groups.

Complete the table with the following in mind:

● Your answers should be based upon your current experiences of one team of which you are a member. I suggest that the team you choose is either the one that you feel has the most prominence in terms of your job or is a team over which you have considerable influence.

● Against each of the ten characteristics you need to mark the chosen team on a basis of 1–5 in the three sections below: 1 is low, 5 is high.

Grades

1   The team has achieved this characteristic.

2   The team is quite good in terms of this characteristic.

3   You are unclear as there is evidence both ways.

4   This is a minor failing of the team.

5   This is a major failing of the team.

Issue

● Summarize very briefly the issue surrounding any grade from 3 to 5.

● Leave the 'Action column' vacant at this stage.

● Compare your scores with another colleague and in particular concentrate on any grades 4 or 5 with a view to discussing likely action.

Action

● Complete the Action column on the basis of this discussion with your colleague.

Characteristics	Grade	Issue	Action
1 Everyone has trust and confidence in everyone else.			
2 All members need to possess skills in leading and following to realize each person's potential.			
3 The working relationship is relaxed, supportive and non-threatening.			
4 The team values and goals are shared and meet everyone's needs, since members were involved in shaping them. These goals are linked with those of other teams.			
5 Each member does everything possible to help the team achieve the goals, and expects everyone else to do the same.			

first time MANAGER

Characteristics	**Grade**	**Issue**	**Action**
6 Expectations are high, but without pressure, thus stretching and accelerating the growth of individuals.			
7 Creativity is prized.			
8 Once processes are agreed, everyone abides by them until, after reflection, it is necessary to change them.			
9 Communication is full and frank.			
10 Hidden agendas are addressed.			

A superteam

A	Achieves

S	Smiles
U	Understands
P	Performs
E	Encourages
R	Reflects

T	Trusts
E	Energizes
A	Aspires
M	Motivates

and so does the team manager.

The Civil list

The Civil checklist for team-builders
Thirty tips. Successful team work is:

1   Everyone pulling in the same direction.

2   Everyone pulling their weight.

3   Always having support available when you want it.

4   Being accepted for what you are, warts and all.

5   Going to do something you've overlooked, and finding it done for you.

6   Getting help when you need it and no interference when you don't.

7   Feeling that it is a pleasure to see your colleagues, at work and socially.

8   Everyone mucking in to retrieve a disaster.

9   Everyone pitching in without complaint when there's a crisis.

10 Enjoying each other's successes, commiserating and supporting each other when setbacks occur.

11 Sharing an exciting vision of the future.

12 Being pleased to get together with your colleagues.

13 Depending on your colleagues to deliver what they promise, so that you know what you have to do and what you don't have to do.

14 Dancing to the same rhythm.

15 A feeling of belonging and of equal value.

16 Knowing what was said will be done, and if it isn't, hearing about it in time to do something about it.

17 Missing someone when they are on leave or are sick.

18 Being able to enjoy everyone's good points, and address their bad ones.

19 Not having to hold anything back; whatever is said is meant and taken constructively.

20 A tree swaying in the wind – individual branches may break off, but the tree stays strong.

21 Sharing the load.

22 The sum of the individuals' capabilities multiplied by the number of individuals.

23 Sometimes carrying, sometimes being carried.

24 All working towards the same targets and beliefs.

25 A level of trust and openness that allows for total communication.

26 Checking out so that you know clearly who is doing what and when.

27 Not having to be asked.

28 Taking care of each other.

29 Looking out for each other.

30 Being able to disagree without being disagreeable.

QUESTIONNAIRE 5
What is my management style?
• •

What role do I think I play in my team?

_____

_____

_____

_____

What role would I like to play?

_____

_____

_____

_____

What do I do positively when managing my team?

_____

_____

_____

_____

What do I need to do now to have a more effective team?

_____

_____

_____

_____

CHAPTER **5**

Am I a motivating manager?

Is it really possible to motivate staff?

The answer is yes, although some theorists may argue that you cannot motivate anybody, people must motivate themselves. I agree that staff do indeed have to be self-motivated in order to work effectively with you, but you can motivate them by the way in which you manage both your interactions with them and their environment. If you *want* to motivate your staff; rather than feel you *have* to motivate them as part of your job, you will be more successful as a manager.

In this chapter I will begin by offering you a questionnaire on 'Are you a motivating manager?' and then take a brief look at some of the theories of motivation and how they can be used to improve your leadership style

QUESTIONNAIRE 6
Am I a motivating manager?

• •

Be honest, how many of the following ten motivating skills do you have? Please tick the 'yes' box if you act on all or part of the statement, or the 'no' box if you do not.

		Yes	No
1	I **listen** to my staff's needs, aspirations frustrations, successes.	☐	☐
2	I **empower** staff to celebrate their skills, empower when I delegate, enabling them to establish practices that create a feeling of belonging.	☐	☐
3	I **appraise** and interview in a two-way, open, honest process, offering feedback and the opportunity for their personal development as well as realistic targets.	☐	☐
4	I **deliver** responses and react positively to new ideas from staff, and wherever possible involve them in decision-making.	☐	☐
5	I **encourage** staff to work in a way that develops their potential and gives them job satisfaction.	☐	☐
6	I **respect** staff with different ideas, attitudes and working practices and respond by recognizing their strengths, even when we agree to differ.	☐	☐
7	I **stimulate** staff into taking risks and trying out new ideas, ensuring that I support them in their success or failure.	☐	☐

8　I **help** staff when they may temporarily be ☐ ☐
　　demotivated, either through not achieving
　　what they want at work, or through family
　　or personal concerns.

9　I try to **inspire** my staff by my positive ☐ ☐
　　attitude, and encourage them to recognize
　　how their work and contributions are valued.

10 I **praise** staff and find it easy to do this ☐ ☐
　　in a genuine way when they have done
　　something well.

Analysis

Now add up all your 'yes' answers

10–8 Yes answers:
　　Brilliant. As a manager you know how to motivate
　　your staff: try training your co-workers.

7–5　Yes answers:
　　You are on the right track, but still need to develop
　　more skills and practices if you really want to be a
　　motivating manager.

4–0　Yes answers:
　　Come on now, you can do better than this. Over the
　　next month try to practise the skills for which you
　　scored a 'no'. Watch the difference in the morale and
　　motivation of your staff.

Leadership to motivate means

L	Listen
E	Empower
A	Appraise
D	Deliver
E	Encourage
R	Respect
S	Stimulate
H	Help
I	Inspire
P	Praise

■ What motivates you?

Your motives are deeply ingrained. They come from childhood experiences, messages, teachings, friends, values, beliefs. There are no simple answers to the question, but try to find them by listing three single words that motivate you.

_____

_____

_____

Do your motives include money? This is an external thing. Money in itself is only a short-term goal achieved. When you receive more money, you will soon become used to it and be driven by wanting to achieve more. If you can identify what would then drive you, that would be your motive.

Maybe you need money to feel secure, pay your bills and maintain your home and standard of living. If so, feeling secure is your motive. Maybe this does not fit you. Perhaps you want money to start up your own business and pursue your leisure and hobbies, travel, or to give to someone else. So your motives could be *independence* (your own boss) or *freedom* (to travel) or *approval* (from others).

Motivating staff

Motivation is how you encourage, attract, influence and induce your staff to work to their full potential, so that they experience a sense of job satisfaction. In order to feel satisfied they will need to be getting what they want. A motive is a state of mind that stems from an unequal balance between what people *want* and what they *have*. Some of your staff may want to work in a different way from the way they do, but may think that they can't or that you won't allow any changes, meaning they have to work in a specific way. They may want to change to flexitime, but feel that you would be adverse to such a work pattern. They may want more responsibility, but feel that what they have is as much as you believe they can handle.

When staff are not motivated they can become aimless, despondent, uninspired, and the job can seem pointless. It is up to you to value their contribution and say so. Also to explain to them why they have to work in certain ways. Explain what the 'pay off' is for them. It may be keeping the job, therefore keeping their standard of living. Or it may be working in a happier and more rewarding way.

You may also be motivated by inner thoughts and drives instilled in you as a child, such as being perfect, pleasing others, hurrying up, being strong, and trying harder. The way you think is how you feel. If you think motivating thoughts you can feel motivated. It's easier than you think.

How can I inspire and motivate staff during a period of change?

As a first-time or long-time manager, you will always be making changes on a small or larger scale. So you need to recognize how best to bring about changes in attitude and behaviour. You will need to motivate your staff so that they can see something they want in the changes that you make.

The word motivator can be interpreted as a 'manager' or 'stringpuller'. Motivated people try to create balance or inner harmony by sometimes changing their behaviour or rationalizing situations, and you will need to be aware of this when introducing change.

Nevertheless, you may have some staff who will not change their behaviour, or who will think irrationally. It is important that you recognize these behavioural patterns as unconscious balancing acts, rather than rational problems that need solving. So much depends on each staff member's wants and desired ends.

To achieve their desires, you will first have to recognize their needs. It is these that will drive them to change their behaviour. This, in turn, satisfies their need to achieve what they want.

Therefore, you must always be aware of the needs of your staff and understand what drives them. They will change their behaviour if they believe that their needs will be satisfied and they can achieve what they want.

Also remember that you must be aware of how people's motives can change from time to time, according to personal pressures, changing values, lifestyles, age and role. Working

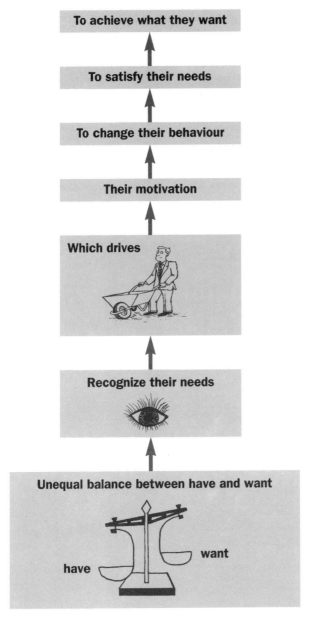

Figure 1

practices that satisfy a young single staff member may not satisfy an older family person. You will need to adapt your management style to suit each individual member of the team.

What ideas have been offered as to how people are motivated?

DOUGLAS MCGREGOR (1906–1964) was a social psychologist and Professor of Management at the Massachusetts Institute of Technology. His basic assumption about the human behaviour that underlies how managers act is known as Theory X and Y.

X-type managers believe that human beings have an inherent dislike of work and will try to avoid it. Therefore managers need to control, direct and punish to achieve their goals.

Y-type managers believe that people do not inherently dislike work and, dependent on how they are managed, it can be either a source of satisfaction or punishment. People will work to their fullest potential if they are empowered.

It was thought that these were two separate sets of attitudes held by managers, rather than both being appropriate for different situations.

Fortunately, most managers today would recognize that from time to time there is a need to control situations, even discipline some individuals, while simultaneously empowering and freeing most of their staff to develop and initiate work within their job role.

ABRAHAM MASLOW, a clinical psychologist, maintained that the strongest motivating factor for people was 'self-actualization', which means realizing your full psychological potential. He initiated the phrase 'A hierachy of human needs'. In order to motivate your staff, you must be aware of their basic needs. Now look at Figure 2.

Figure 2
In order to
motivate staff,
recognize their
human needs.

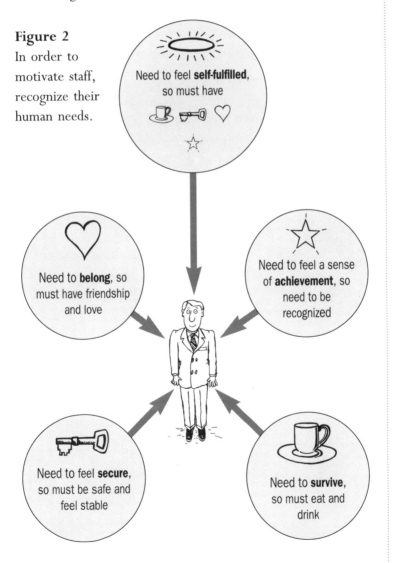

Need to feel **self-fulfilled**, so must have

Need to **belong**, so must have friendship and love

Need to feel a sense of **achievement**, so need to be recognized

Need to feel **secure**, so must be safe and feel stable

Need to **survive**, so must eat and drink

Need to survive

As a first-time or long-time manager you should be aware that people have basic physiological requirements of hunger or thirst and physical comfort and these physiological needs ought to be satisfied in the workplace. You should ensure they have comfortable working areas, breaks away from their work, natural lighting and adequate heating.

Need to feel secure

Your staff will also need to feel safe: there should be security and stability in your work setting. As we become aware of more and more cases of violence and aggression both in our schools and within industry, it is important that people do feel safe at work.

Need to belong

Do your staff feel as though they belong? Or do they feel they are being used? They need the support of affection, friendship and love within their working environment. In order to motivate your staff, you must address their basic needs before they can move on to being highly motivated individuals, working with you and the organization.

Need to feel a sense of achievement

If you have ☕ 🔑 and ♡ , then a sense of achievement will follow. Feeling recognized is great for everyone, including you, so praise, praise, praise!

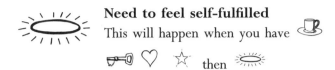

Need to feel self-fulfilled
This will happen when you have ☕

🗝 ♡ ☆ then ⛅

FREDERICK HERZBERG, a psychologist and Professor of Management at the University of Utah, identified two aspects of motivation theory: Hygiene factors and Motivating factors. See Figure 3.

Motivating factors	Hygiene factors
	or
Achievement and recognition for accomplishments	Working conditions
	Relationships
More responsibility	Money, status, security, policies
Personal growth	Clear administrative procedures

Figure 3

Hygiene factors by themselves do not motivate your staff, but their *absence* can *demotivate*.

Praise, praise, praise!

Staff grow with praise and shrivel with criticism.

People are your greatest resource, manage them so that they grow towards you, not shrivel away from you.

The greatest motivators have fun with their team. Prick the pomposity bubble, be spontaneous, natural and enjoy your and others' humour. This will help your staff to feel a sense of belonging to the group.

There are no easy answers to motivating your staff, each one will have individual needs and aspirations and you will have to be highly trained in sensitivity, leadership and people skills to keep up the level of involvement required. However, the one sure way is to remember the questionnaire you have addressed, which can be simply remembered as the word PRAISE:

P	Praise and Persuade
R	React and Respect
A	Appraise and Appreciate
I	Involve and Inspire
S	Stimulate and Support
E	Encourage and Empower

Ten motivating messages

M	Manage with realistic and achievable targets
O	Organize a safe and secure environment
T	Trust staff to be responsible
I	Involve your staff so that they feel they belong
V	Value good performance and staff achievements
A	Allow staff maximum freedom to do their job
T	Take time to listen and explain instructions
I	Increase in salary is only a short-term motivator
O	Overpraising cheapens the message
N	Nurture staff's basic human needs

QUESTIONNAIRE 7
What is my management style?

● ●

Having read this chapter, what have you discovered?

How do I motivate my staff? By _____

_____

_____

_____

_____

_____

What attributes do I already possess
in order to motivate them? _____

_____

_____

_____

_____

_____

Which new ideas do I need to consider?

_____

_____

_____

_____

_____

_____

What have I learned from this chapter?

_____

_____

_____

_____

What do I now need to do to be a more successful, motivating manager?

_____

_____

_____

_____

CHAPTER 6

Ways to inspire and motivate staff during a period of change

There are numerous pressures on you as a leader, and there will certainly be pressure when you have to bring about some form of change. If you do this well you will be a good leader. In order to succeed, you will need to consider two elements of the change:

1   The quality of the kind of change that you wish to instigate, and whether it is seen as something good or bad. Remember, staff will be looking and listening to see or hear if it has anything in it that motivates them – more influence, more status, more job satisfaction – and, as explained in the last chapter, looking for their individual needs to be met.

2 The quality of how you implement the change.
   If you take what seems forever to make decisions about
   the personnel involved, where people will be located,
   who does what and by when, then staff will reject the
   idea. Equally, if you do it too quickly without adequate
   consultation, you will also get resentment. How you
   implement the change is vital, even when the change you
   are making is seen as a good idea and offers a positive
   improvement of the working conditions or roles. Never
   underestimate emotions when managing change. The
   following window demonstrates the emotions that can
   emerge, and how you need to work towards Active
   Acceptance.

Feelings are facts!

The way people feel is a fact, and you will need to manage them
in a way that creates positive feelings about your objectives.

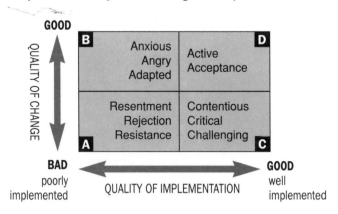

You will need to consider how good or bad the quality of the
change is perceived as being; simultaneously you must ensure
that there is a positive quality in the way that it is implemented.

● If it is seen as a bad change and poorly implemented, staff will reject the change, feeling resentment and resistance to it (**A**).

● If it is seen as a change for the better (good) but poorly implemented, staff will become anxious, angry or adapted (**B**).

● If it is seen as a bad change but well implemented, staff will be critical, contentious and challenging (**C**).

● What you have to aim for is change for the better, well implemented, so that staff are actively accepting (**D**).

How to motivate people when making and introducing changes

You manage through constant change. Can you recall a time in your life when some kind of change was not taking place? Staff leaving, joining, deadlines to meet, staff being ill, changing routines, changing policies, changing rooms and roles. While some staff will always welcome change, others will always resist it. What you need to work towards is getting your staff to embrace change, not resist it. Most of your staff will go with you if you are a skilled leader and manager and consider the following suggestions.

Your employees need to be made aware of the current overall situation within the organization, so you will have to AUDIT THE CURRENT SITUATION in order to pass this information on to them. Ask yourself who does what and what are the outcomes of present practices.

You will need a CLEAR VISION OF THE POSITIVE OUT-COMES for all concerned. That means:

It could be that if present practices continue, the eventual effect on the organization will be detrimental. If this is the case, then say so. An organization that is not functioning efficiently will certainly result in demotivated staff, and, possibly the worst scenario, the loss of jobs.

Show the INDIVIDUAL BENEFITS that will result from the intended changes, encouraging staff to see, for example, the greater job security, more flexibility in working hours, pleasanter working conditions or greater job satisfaction that the new system will bring.

You will need to consider your staff's ROLE, RESPONSIBILITIES and REWARDS.

Have a STAFF DEVELOPMENT PLAN to assist with their

- Role change
- New duties
- Responsibilities
- Learning
- Personal action plan

Find RESOURCES FOR THE SUPPORT NEEDED to manage the transition for:

● The giving of information

● The necessary accommodation

● The management support and time needed to interview staff

● Staff development initiatives.

Establish a MENTORING/BUDDYING or COACHING system. Let staff choose someone they think can support them through the period of change. This may be a manager or colleague with whom they think they can work and so become actively accepting of the changes needed.

How to set about making changes

It is vital that you are on firm ground and not in a swamp. By that I mean that you talk in terms of time – now, this week, next month, in six months, in a year, not sometime. Also, you have to consider who needs to do what. I, You, We ... *not* someone!

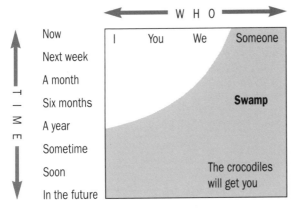

Now imagine that you have to bring in management restructure or flexi-time. Identify five steps that would ensure active acceptance.

1 _____

_____

_____

_____

2 _____

_____

_____

_____

3 _____

_____

_____

_____

4 _____

_____

_____

_____

5 _____

_____

_____

_____

Remember that successful change is all about …

C	Checking reasons
H	Holding present quality practices
A	Anchoring groups
N	Negotiating
G	Going for it
E	Explaining why

QUESTIONNAIRE 8
How do I implement changes?
● ●

1   What change do I want to make?

_____

_____

_____

2   Why?

_____

_____

_____

3   What outcomes do I want to achieve?

_____

_____

_____

4   How will I start the change process?

_____

_____

_____

_____

_____

5   What information will I communicate to staff?

_____

_____

_____

_____

_____

6   What aspects of the change are negotiable?

_____

_____

_____

_____

_____

7   What aspects of the change are not negotiable?

_____

_____

_____

_____

_____

8   Who do I want to do what?

Who _____   What _____

_____   _____

_____   _____

_____   _____

_____   _____

9   What are the drawbacks of the change?

_____

_____

_____

_____

_____

_____

10 What are the benefits of the change?

_____

_____

_____

_____

_____

_____

What do I need to do to implement change well?

1 Explain the reasons for the change.

2 Aim for ownership through Active Acceptance.

3 Encourage constructive criticism and discourage compliance.

4 Involve people in as many stages as is possible and wise.

5 Seek advice from experienced staff regarding potential barriers.

6 Work to a manageable time scale.

7 Establish what is negotiable and what is not negotiable.

8 Empower staff to contribute in negotiations and communicate your progress through active reviewing meetings.

9 Keep to your promise of decisions to be made by certain times as staff pace themselves to your deadlines. They become resentful when you do not come to a decision.

10 Learn to reduce pressures on yourself so that you can manage change and your job effectively

How can I reduce pressures on myself?

While managing change for other people, you will also need to consider how change affects you. You are probably prepared to work hard to be a good leader, but you are also likely to have recognized that there are many pressures on you. As a leader and manager you will be aware of the many complexities of people's behaviours and feelings, including your own. So it is important that you now consider how you can cope with the pressures of being a leader.

First of all, celebrate the things that you already have going for you as a leader. Your influence on working practices and procedures, your opportunity for creativity, your ability to implement new ways of working, your freedom to plan your time and working patterns, your skills to improve people's way of life and your power to change things. That is quite a pleasant state to be in.

Believe in what you are doing and recognize the reasons behind the pressures on yourself. Think: are they really pressures or are they exciting opportunities? You need some pressure. You could suffer from 'rust out' if you don't have enough, or 'burn out' if you have too much, so work towards the power of balance.

Go for small successes rather than big failures. Learn to laugh at your mistakes, but learn from them. Ask for support when you need it. You need to be a strong manager to show vulnerability. Almost all people are amazingly kind if you ask for help or assistance.

If you believe that there is such a thing as psychosomatic illness, then there can also be psychosomatic wellness. So think healthy rather than sickly. Look towards your own health and well-being. You are no good as a leader or to anyone if you are physically ill or mentally exhausted. So stop playing the martyr and take those lunch breaks. Who are you trying to impress by having sandwiches at your desk? If you are doing this, then you are not planning your time successfully. Of course it's fine now and again to meet deadlines, and it can be exhilarating, but not as a constant pattern of behaviour.

Try to work smarter, not harder. Take breaks for exercise, eat sensibly, avoid caffeine. Be in control of your drinking and smoking habits. Recharge your batteries, restore your energy with the right kind of sleep, or use homoeopathic remedies such as guarana for fatigue.

It's OK to feel emotions, make some 'selfish' time for yourself. Enjoy your sexuality. Enjoy your leisure. Remember you have no leisure time unless you have worktime. Now that you can recognize your management style, concentrate on your natural attributes and work towards developing those in which you now know you are deficient. Knowing your cameo of characteristics will give you a greater understanding of your own and your staff's preferred style of working. So you can avoid pressurizing yourself and others by expecting them to work in a way that is uncomfortable for them, or out of character.

Now you can relieve the pressure on yourself as a team leader by discovering your team's natural roles and giving them work accordingly. Always empower your team members when delegating. Give them all the facts and power that go with the job. Support them when things go wrong. Try to develop trust in your team. This relieves pressure for all of you. Address any conflict when it arises rather than letting it fester.

Pressure will be reduced considerably if you know how to motivate yourself and your staff. Find out what makes your staff tick and whenever possible try to give them what they want or desire in job terms.

If you always do what you've always done, you'll always get what you've always got – so try behaving differently. Above all, have some fun!

CONCLUSION

So, what happened? Were you surprised, delighted, annoyed, irritated or amused by your scores and insights? You have worked through many different ideas and approaches. Some will have felt comfortable and acceptable, while others may have made you feel uneasy, or created disbelief.

The important thing is not so much your scores, research or evidence, but what you have learned about yourself during the process, recognizing and celebrating your attributes while considering other ways of thinking or behaving towards your staff.

Now let us look at the cumulative summary of your management style

Cumulative summary of my management style

Complete the following statement from each of the chapter summaries, in order to gather together your wide and varied approaches to management. To do this, refer back to 'What is my management style' at the end of chapters 1–5.

1 My Civil cameo of characteristics is: _____

_____

2 My leadership style is: _____

My strengths are: _____

_____

I need to consider: _____

_____

_____

3 My lifestyle scores are: P_____   S _____   F _____

My strengths are: _____

_____

I need to consider: _____

_____

_____

4 My joint cameo and lifestyle is: P_____   S _____   F _____

This indicates that I _____

_____

_____

5   My preferred role in teams is: _____

My strengths as a team leader are: _____

_____

I need to consider: _____

_____

_____

6   I motivate my staff by: _____

_____

_____

My strengths are: _____

_____

I need to consider: _____

_____

_____

7   I need to consider the following points when implementing change: _____

_____

_____

The best way to get my staff actively to accept change is by:

_____

_____

_____

_____

What have you deduced from these explorations?

I have learned that my positive attributes are: _____

·   _____

·   _____

·   _____

I have learned that my negative aspects are: _____

_____

·   _____

·   _____

I will change: _____

_____

_____

_____

·   _____

I will continue: _____

_____

_____

_____

_____

The most enlightening thing for me after reading this book is:

_____

_____

_____

_____

I hope the book has helped you towards understanding your-self and recognizing the differences between people, appreci-ating the need for different personality types within your organization. Maybe you now know why you work better with some staff and not so well with others.

You will recognize what motivates some of your staff and maybe work towards managing in a more successful way. When, or if, you ever have to implement any changes you will be able to recognize the importance of the need for staff to know why change is necessary and how to implement it so that they actively accept the new measures necessary.

Finally, if you have taken the trouble to read this book, you are well on the way to becoming a good manager. Congratulations!